Gospel songs
for
Alto *Hugh Tracey* Kalimba

Ondřej Šárek

Contents

Introduction

Sacred music is often played. But there is a problem when the player wants to play a solo on a Alto Hugh Tracey Kalimba. For the reason the book was written. You can find here 23 gospels and spirituals. And now you can start playing, singing and worshiping our Lord.

How to read tablature

Kalimba

Play the lammella no.1
by the thumb of left hand

Play the lammella no.4
by the thumb of right hand.

Play lammellas no.1 and 6
by thumbs of both hands.

K.

Play lammellas no.2 and 4
by the thumb of right hand.

Play arpeggio
lammellas no.1, 3 and 5
by the thumb of left hand

Play the lammella no.7
by the thumb of left hand.
and play lammellas no.2 and 4
by the thumb of right hand

Lamella chart

K.

All Night, All Day

arr: Ondřej Šárek

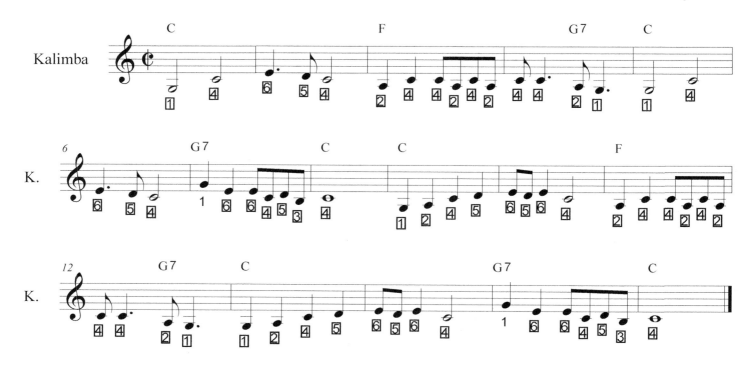

All Night, All Day

arr: Ondřej Šárek

Amazing Grace

arr: Ondřej Šárek

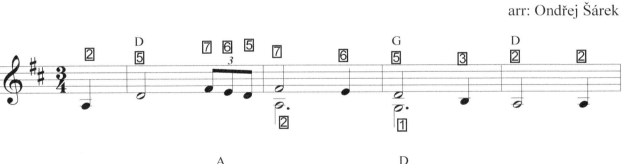

Amazing Grace

arr: Ondřej Šárek

Score

Amazing Grace

arr: Ondřej Šárek

Score

Angel Band

arr: Ondřej Šárek

Score

Angel Band

arr: Ondřej Šárek

Kalimba

Score

The Angel Rolled The Stone Away

arr: Ondřej Šárek

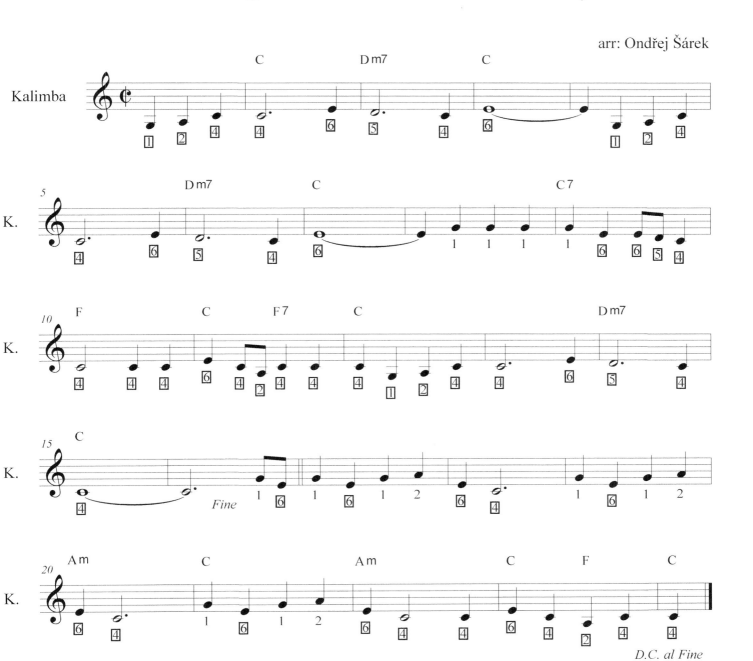

Score

The Angel Rolled The Stone Away

arr: Ondřej Šárek

Score

The Angel Rolled The Stone Away

arr: Ondřej Šárek

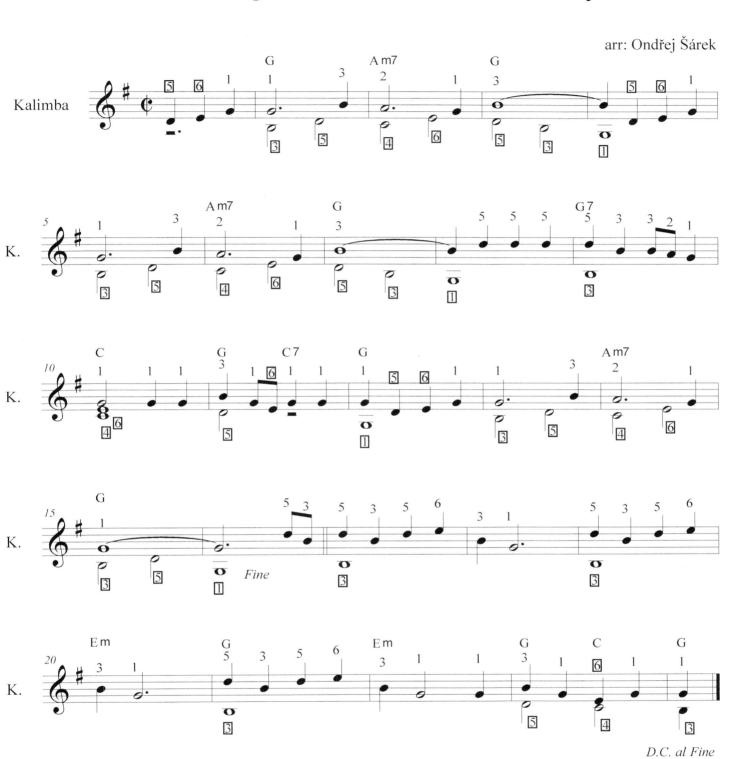

Score

Are You Washed in the Blood

arr: Ondřej Šárek

Kalimba

Score

Are You Washed in the Blood

arr: Ondřej Šárek

Kalimba

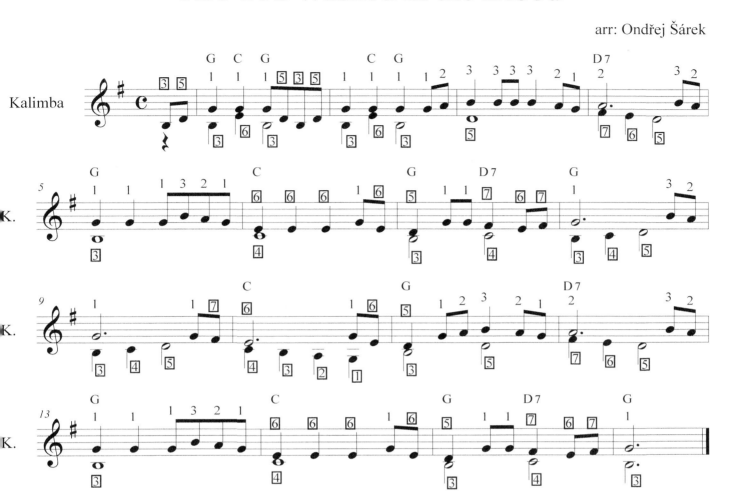

Score

Crying Holy

arr: Ondřej Šárek

Score

Crying Holy

arr: Ondřej Šárek

Score

Gimme Dat Ol'Time Religion

arr: Ondřej Šárek

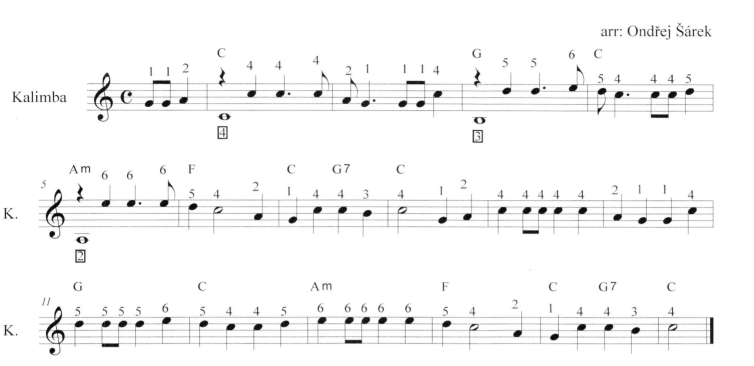

Score

Gimme Dat Ol'Time Religion

arr: Ondřej Šárek

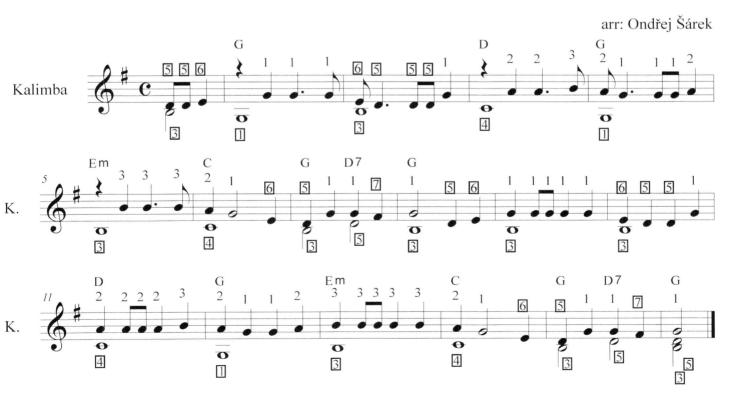

Go, Tell It On The Mountains

arr: Ondřej Šárek

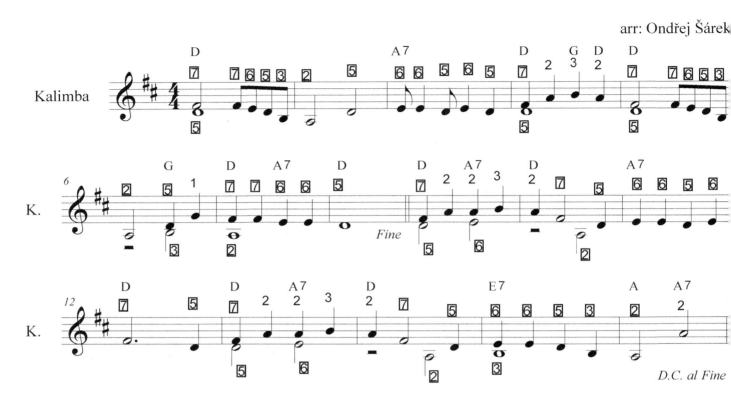

Go, Tell It On The Mountains

arr: Ondřej Šárek

Heav'n

arr: Ondřej Šárek

Kalimba

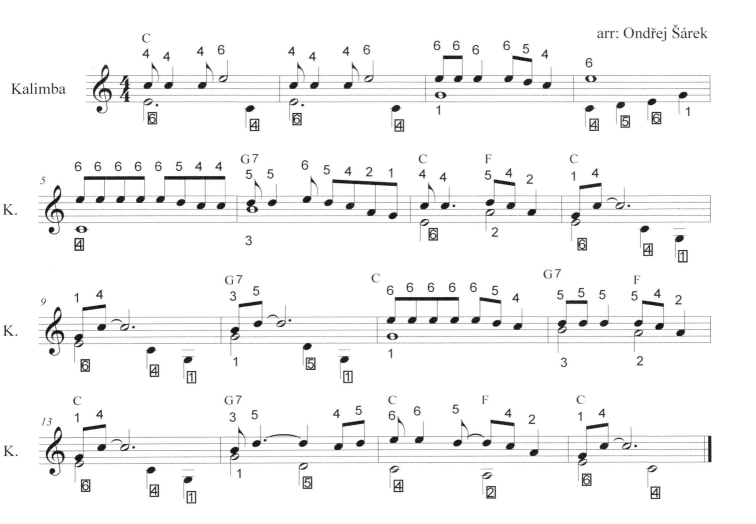

Heav'n

arr: Ondřej Šárek

Kalimba

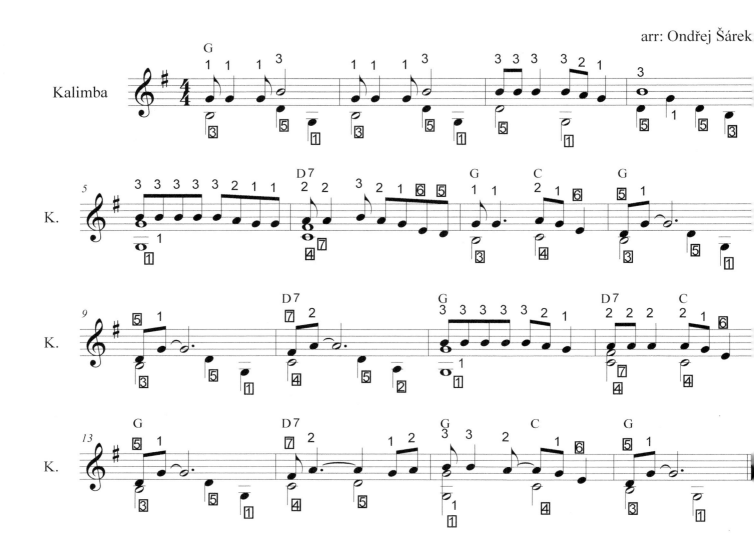

Score

He's Got the Whole World

arr: Ondřej Šáre

Kalimba

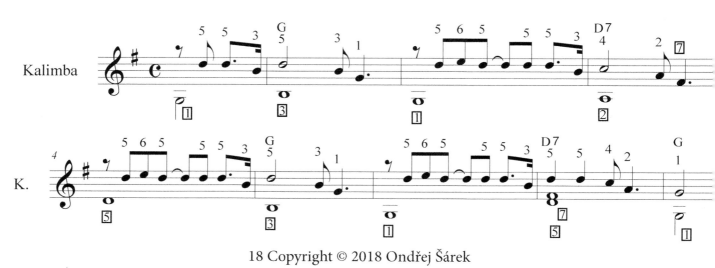

I'm Gonna Sing

arr: Ondřej Šárek

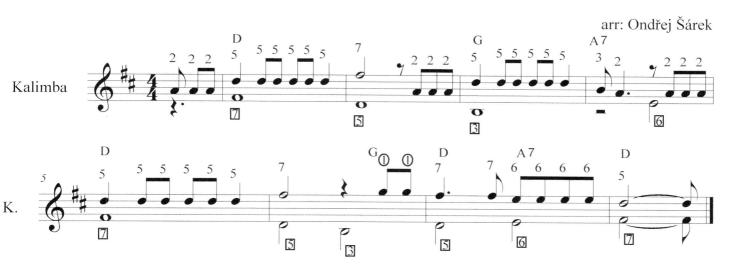

I'm Gonna Sing

arr: Ondřej Šárek

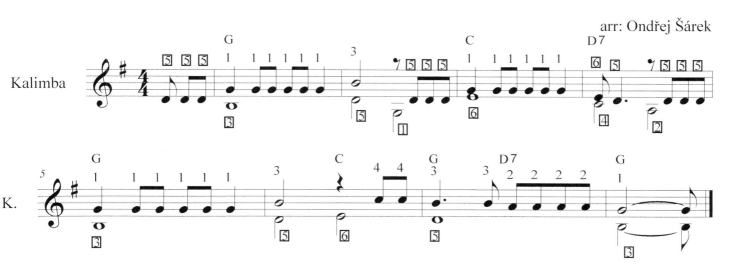

Kum ba yah

Score

arr: Ondřej Šárek

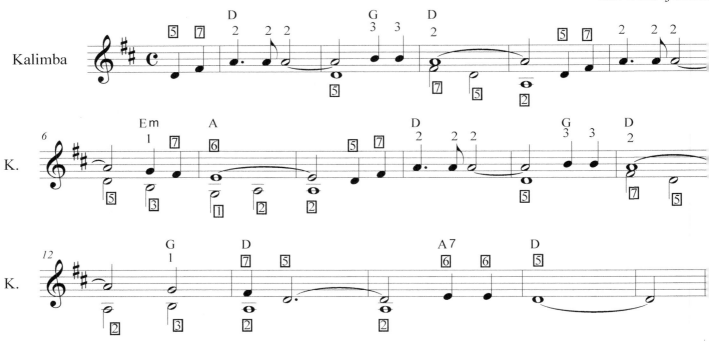

Kum ba yah

Score

arr: Ondřej Šárek

Mary Had A Baby

arr: Ondřej Šárek

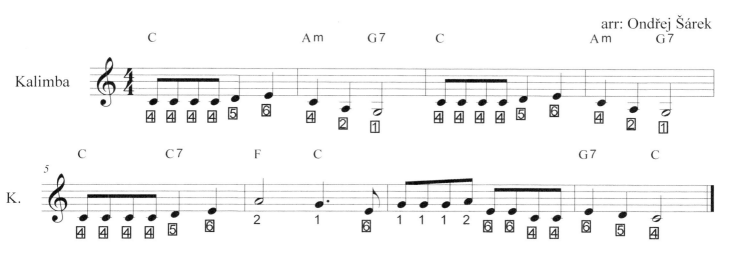

Mary Had A Baby

arr: Ondřej Šárek

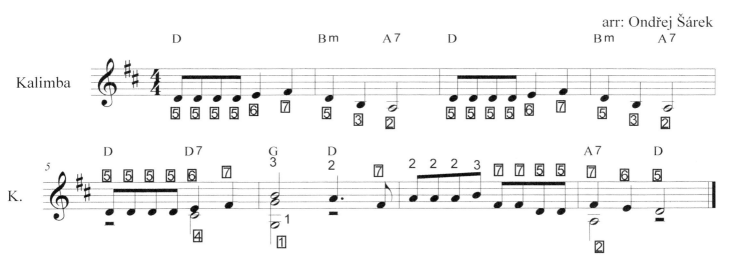

Mary Had A Baby

arr: Ondřej Šárek

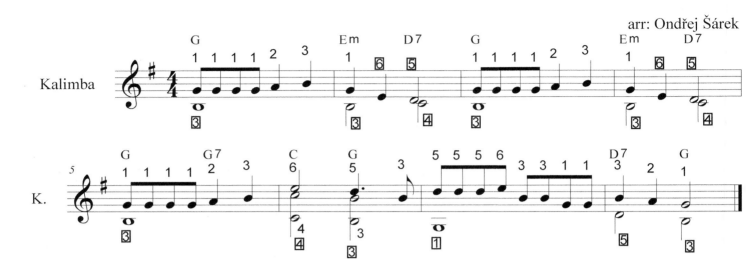

Michael, Row The boat Ashore

Score

arr: Ondřej Šárek

Score

Michael, Row The boat Ashore

arr: Ondřej Šárek

Kalimba

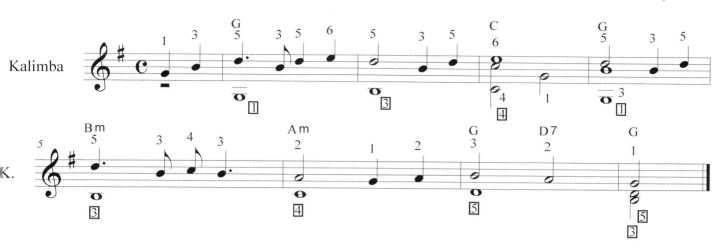

Oh Freedom

arr: Ondřej Šárek

Kalimba

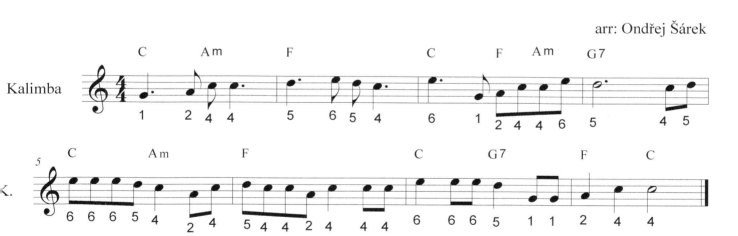

Oh Freedom

arr: Ondřej Šárek

Kalimba

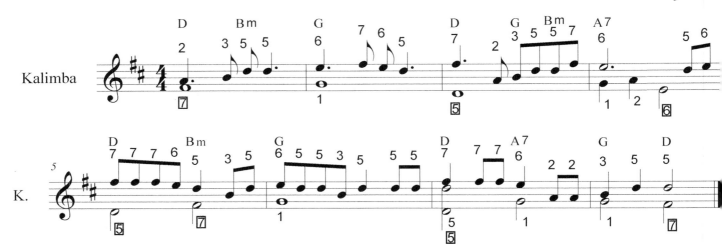

Oh Freedom

arr: Ondřej Šárek

Kalimba

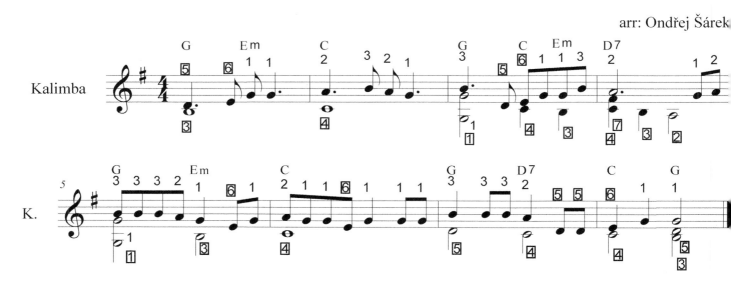

Oh, Sinner man

arr: Ondřej Šárek

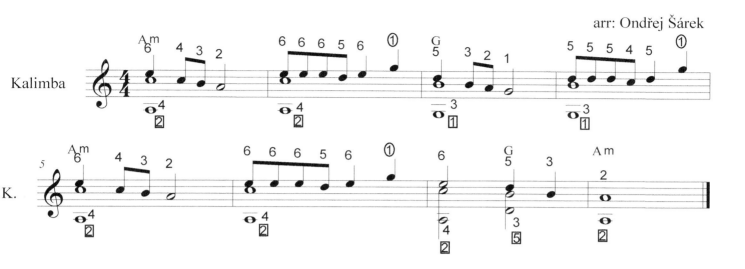

Kalimba

Oh, Sinner man

arr: Ondřej Šárek

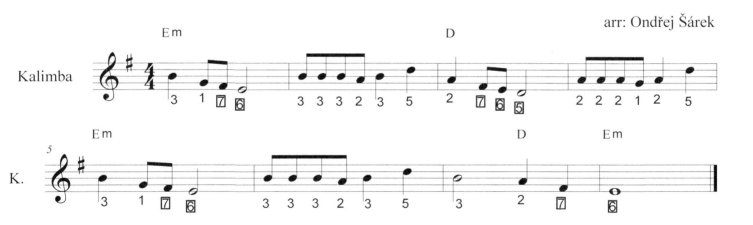

Kalimba

Oh, When The Saints

arr: Ondřej Šárek

Kalimba

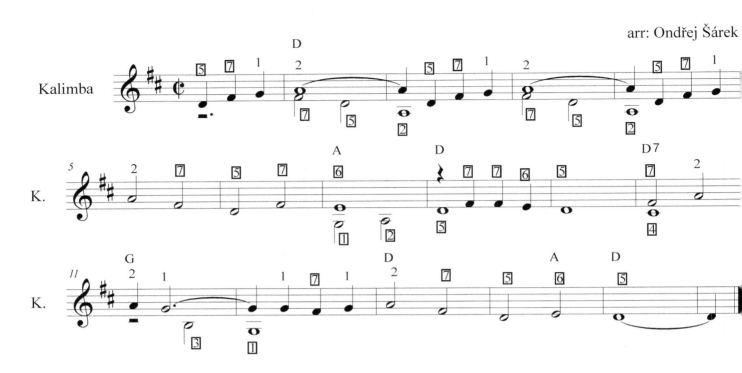

Score

Oh, When The Saints

arr: Ondřej Šárel

Kalimba

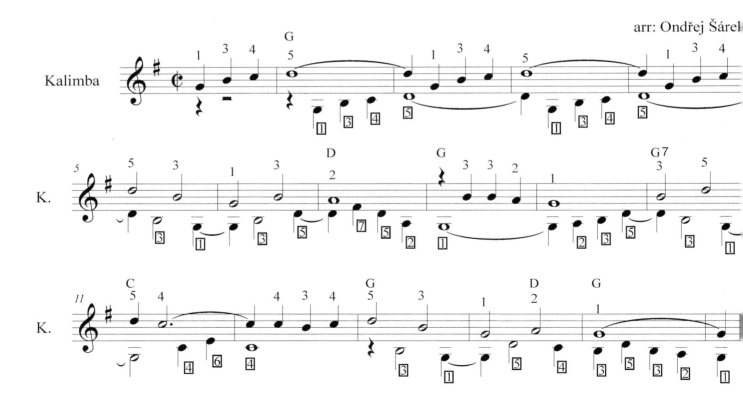

Rock My Soul

arr: Ondřej Šárek

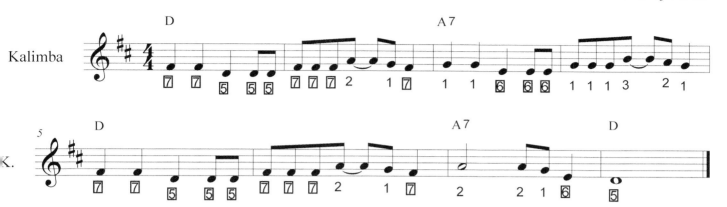

Rock My Soul

arr: Ondřej Šárek

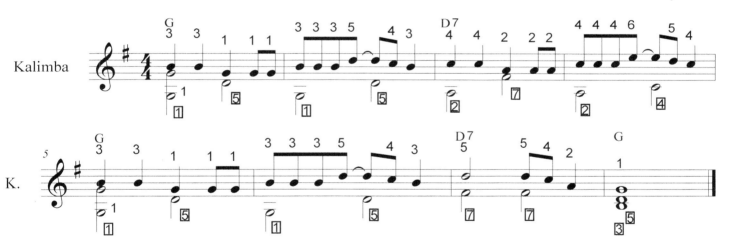

Singin' With A Sword In My Hand

arr: Ondřej Šárek

Singin' With A Sword In My Hand

arr: Ondřej Šárek

Singin' With A Sword In My Hand

arr: Ondřej Šárek

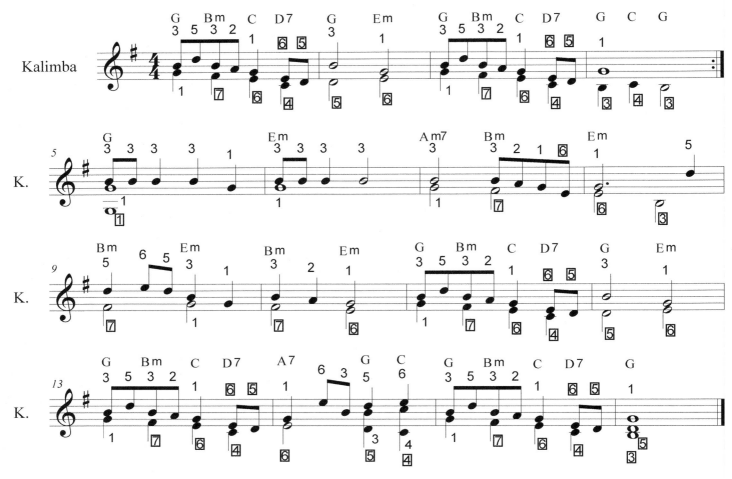

Steal Away

arr: Ondřej Šárek

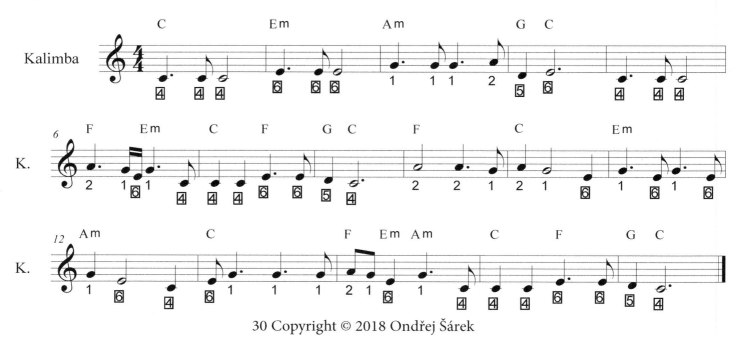

Steal Away

arr: Ondřej Šárek

Kalimba

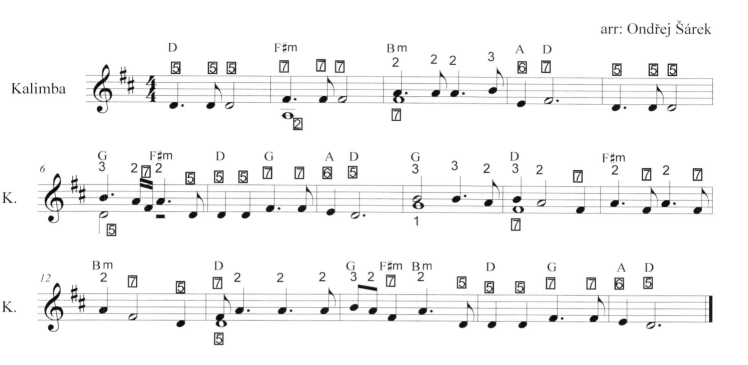

Steal Away

arr: Ondřej Šárek

Kalimba

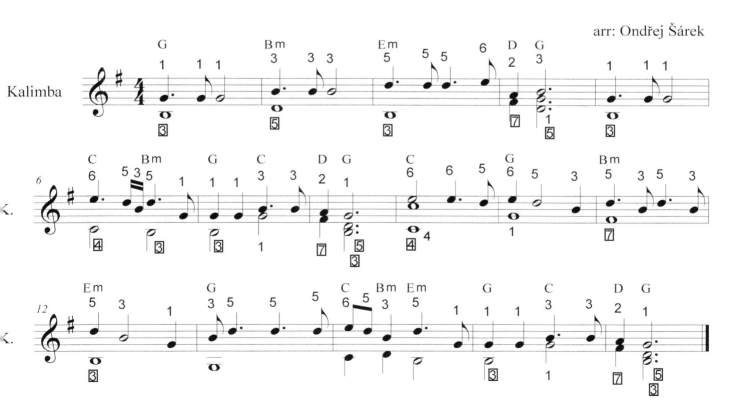

Swing Low, Sweet Chariot

arr: Ondřej Šárek

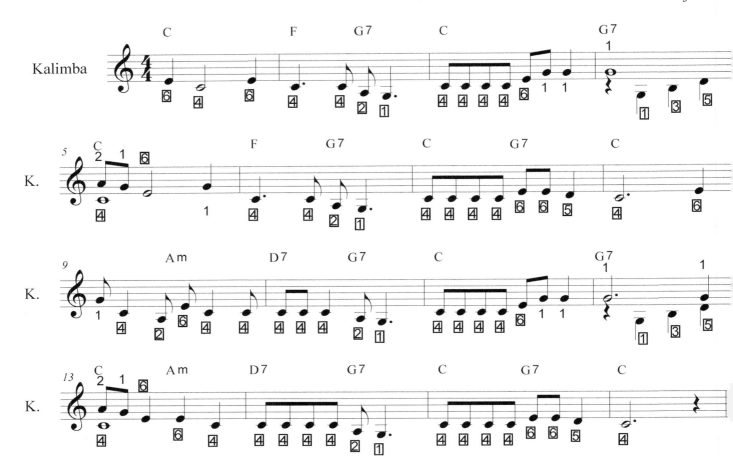

Swing Low, Sweet Chariot

arr: Ondřej Šárek

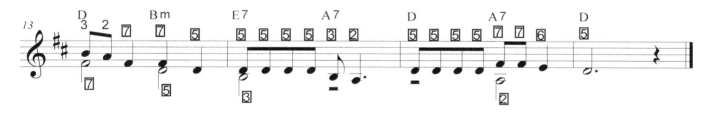

Swing Low, Sweet Chariot

arr: Ondřej Šárek

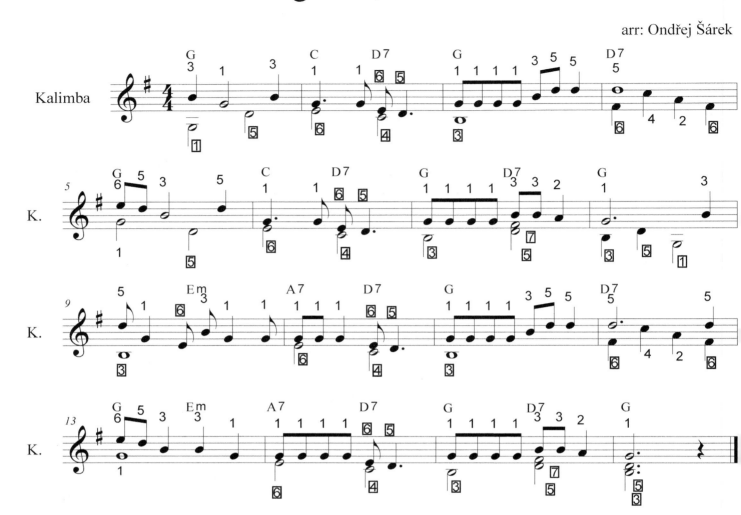

Score

Wayfaring Stranger

arr: Ondřej Šárek

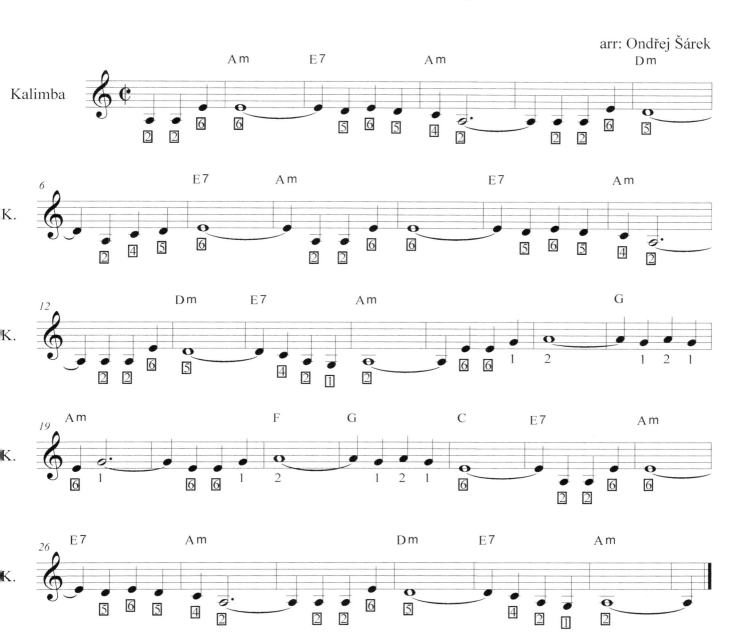

Score

Wayfaring Stranger

arr: Ondřej Šáre

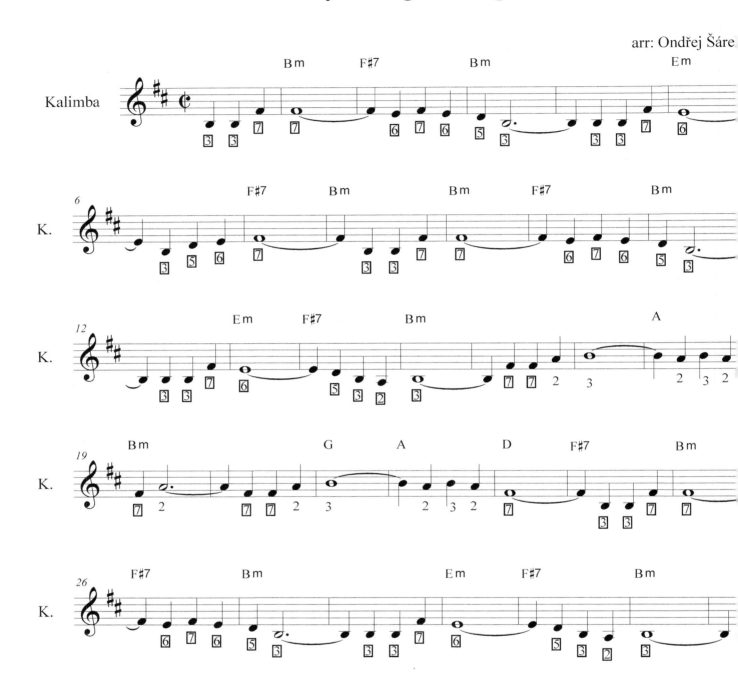

Wayfaring Stranger

Score

arr: Ondřej Šárek

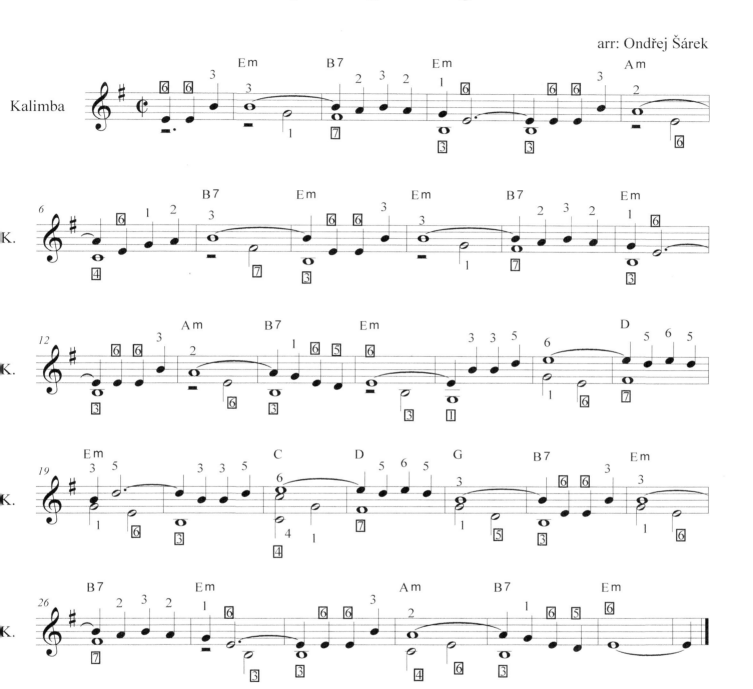

Score

Were You There When They Crucified My Lord?

arr: Ondřej Šárek

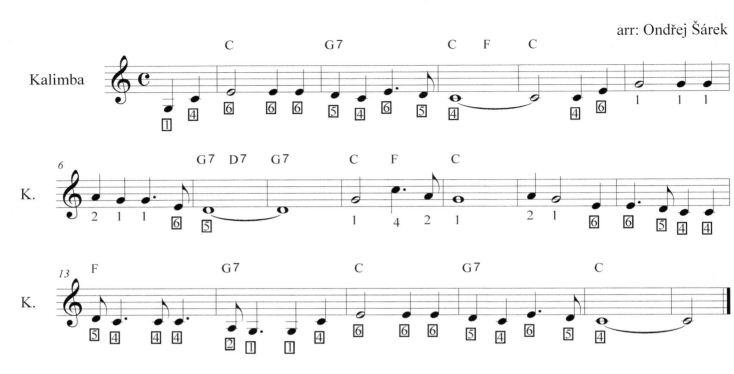

Score

Were You There When They Crucified My Lord?

arr: Ondřej Šárek

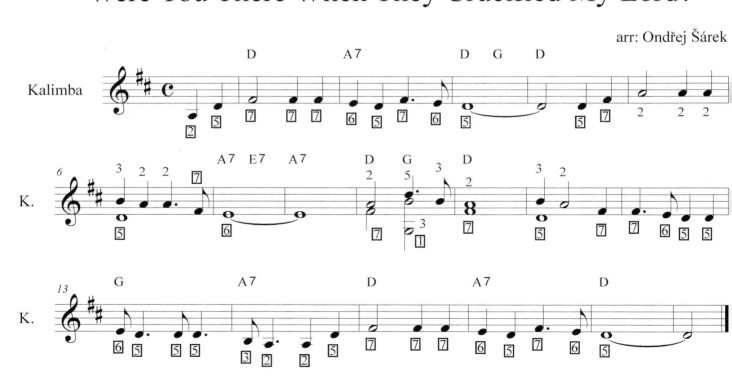

Were You There When They Crucified My Lord?

arr: Ondřej Šárek

Kalimba

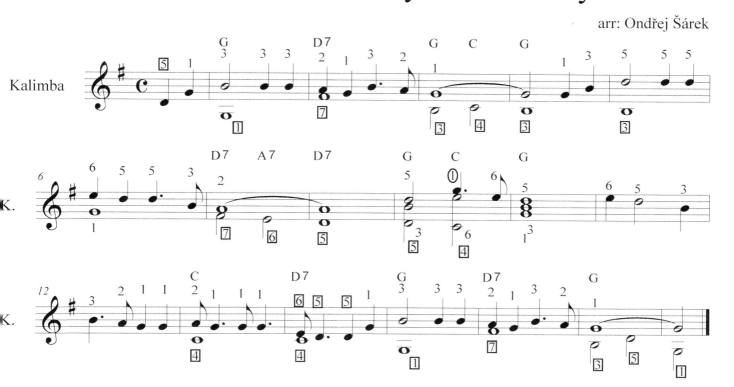

DADGAD Guitar

Czech Medieval DADGAD Guitar
The canons for DADGAD Guitar
Fingerpicking DADGAD Guitar Solo
The Czech Lute for DADGAD Guitar
Gregorian chant for DADGAD Guitar
Gregorian chant for flatpicking DADGAD Guitar
Gospel DADGAD Guitar Solos
Notebook for Anna Magdalena Bach and DADGAD Guitar
Czech Renaissance folk songs for DADGAD Guitar
Robert Burns songs for DADGAD Guitar

EADEAE Guitar

Fingerpicking EADEAE Guitar Solo

CGDGCD (Orkney tuning) Guitar

Gospel CGDGCD Guitar Solos
Notebook for Anna Magdalena Bach and CGDGCD Guitar
Gregorian chant for flatpicking CGDGCD Guitar
Fingerpicking CGDGCD Guitar Solo

EADGBE Guitar

Czech Medieval EADGBE Guitar
Gregorian chant for flatpicking EADGBE Guitar
The canons for EADGBE Guitar
The Czech Lute for EADGBE Guitar
Czech Renaissance folk songs for EADGBE Guitar
Robert Burns songs for EADGBE Guitar
18 Dance Tunes from Caslav Region for EADGBE Guitar
Czech Hymnbook for EADGBE Guitar
18 popular Czech Minuet for EADGBE Guitar

DADGBD (Double drop D tuning) Guitar

Gospel Double drop D tuning Guitar Solos
Notebook for Anna Magdalena Bach and Double drop D tuning Guitar

DADGBE (Drop D tuning) Guitar

Gospel Drop D tuning Guitar Solos
Notebook for Anna Magdalena Bach and Drop D tuning Guitar
Fingerpicking Drop D tuning Guitar Solo
Gregorian chant for flatpicking Drop D tuning Guitar
Robert Burns songs for Drop D tuning Guitar

Cut Capo (Partial Capo) Guitar

Cut capo flatpicking guitar songbook Gospel and Hymns I.
Cut capo flatpicking guitar songbook Gospel and Hymns II.
Cut capo flatpicking guitar songbook Christmas Carols
Cut capo flatpicking guitar songbook Jewish songs
Cut capo flatpicking guitar songbook Gregorian chant
Cut capo flatpicking guitar songbook Children's Songs

G tuning (gDGBD) Banjo

Czech Medieval G tuning Banjo
Classical music for Clawhammer G tuning Banjo
Gregorian chant for G tuning Banjo

Mandolin

Czech Medieval Mandolin
Gregorian chant for flatpicking Mandolin
Czech Renaissance folk songs for Mandolin
Classical music for Mandolin
Christmas Carols for Crosspicking Mandolin
Robert Burns songs for Mandolin
Compositions for Mandolin
18 Dance Tunes from Caslav Region for Mandolin
Fingerpicking Mandolin or GDAE Ukulele Solo
Notebook for Anna Magdalena Bach and Fingerpicking Mandolin or GDAE Ukulele
10 songs from the years 1899-1920 for Mandolin
Czech Hymnbook for Mandolin
Boogie woogie patterns for Mandolin
Gospel for Mandolin

Mandola or Tenor Banjo or Tenor Guitar (CGDA)

Classical music for Mandola or Tenor Banjo
18 Dance Tunes from Caslav Region for Mandola or Tenor Banjo
Robert Burns songs for Mandola or Tenor Banjo
Gregorian chant for Mandola or Tenor Banjo
Fingerpicking Mandola or Tenor Banjo
10 songs from the years 1899-1920 for CGDA Mandola
Czech Hymnbook for CGDA Mandola
Boogie woogie patterns for CGDA Mandola
Christmas Carols for Crosspicking Mandola or Tenor Banjo
Compositions for CGDA Mandola
Romantic Pieces by František Max Kníže for fingerpicking CGDA Tenor Guitar
Classical music for fingerpicking CGDA Tenor Guitar
Cut capo 2220 for CGDA tenor banjo, tenor guitar or mandola
Gospel for CGDA Mandola or Tenor Banjo

Irish (GDAD) Bouzouki

Christmas Carols for Crosspicking GDAD Bouzouki
Classical music for GDAD Bouzouki
Czech Renaissance folk songs for GDAD Bouzouki
Josef Pekárek *Two Hanakian operas* for GDAD Bouzouki
Robert Burns songs for GDAD Bouzouki
18 Dance Tunes from Caslav Region for GDAD Bouzouki
Gregorian chant for GDAD Bouzouki
Compositions for GDAD Bouzouki
Gospel GDAD Bouzouki Solos
10 songs from the years 1899-1920 for GDAD Bouzouki
Czech Hymnbook for GDAD Bouzouki
Boogie woogie patterns for GDAD Bouzouki

Duet for Mandolin and other instrument

Notebook for Anna Magdalena Bach for Mandolin and instrument from the mandolin family
Notebook for Anna Magdalena Bach for Mandolin and EADGBE Guitar
Notebook for Wolfgang for Mandolin and instrument from the mandolin family
Notebook for Wolfgang for Mandolin and EADGBE Guitar

New Ukulele books

For C tuning ukulele
Classics for Ukulele (MB)
Ukulele Bluegrass Solos (MB)
Antonin Dvorak: Biblical Songs
Irish tunes for all ukulele
Gospel Ukulele Solos
Gregorian chant for Ukulele
The Czech Lute for Ukulele
Romantic Pieces by Frantisek Max Knize
for Ukulele
Notebook for Anna Magdalena Bach and
Ukulele
Open Tunings for Ukulel (MB)
Robert Burns songs for ukulele
Jewish songs for C tuning ukulele
Campanella style songbook for beginner:
C tuning ukulele
Antonín Dvořák: opera The Jacobin for
ukulele
Leopold Mozart's Notebook for Wolfgang
Arranged for Ukulele (MB)
The canons for one or two ukuleles
Solo and Variations for ukulele volume 1.,
2., 3.
Czech Medieval Ukulele
Christmas Carols for ukulele
Harmonics for ukulele
43 Ghiribizzi by Niccolo Paganini for
Ukulele
Christmas Carols for Clawhammer ukulele
Gospel Clawhammer ukulele Solos
Czech Renaissance folk songs for Ukulele
Classical music for Clawhammer Ukulele
Christmas Carols for Crosspicking Ukulele
Josef Pekárek Two Hanakian operas
for Ukulele
How to play on three ukulele
simultaneously
Clawhammer solo for Ukulele
Gospel Crosspicking Ukulele Solos
48 Fingerstyle Studies for Ukulele
Compositions for ukulele
18 Dance Tunes from Caslav Region for
Ukulele
Francisco Tárrega for Ukulele (MB)
10 songs from the years 1899-1920 for
Ukulele
Czech Hymnbook for Ukulele
Campanella style songbook
for intermediate

For C tuning with low G
Irish tunes for all ukulele
Gospel Ukulele low G Solos
Antonin Dvorak: Biblical Songs: for
Ukulele with low G
Gregorian chant for Ukulele with low G
The Czech Lute for Ukulele with low G
Romantic Pieces by Frantisek Max Knize
for Ukulele with low G
Notebook for Anna Magdalena Bach and
Ukulele with low G
Robert Burns songs for ukulele with low G
Jewish songs for ukulele with low G
Campanella style songbook for beginner:
ukulele with low G
Czech Medieval Ukulele with low G
Christmas Carols for ukulele with low G
Fingerpicking solo for Ukulele with low G
43 Ghiribizzi by Niccolo Paganini for
Ukulele with low G
Christmas Carols for Crosspicking Ukulele
with low G
Czech Renaissance folk songs for Ukulele
with low G
Gospel Crosspicking Ukulele with low G
Solos
Josef Pekárek Two Hanakian operas for
Ukulele with low G
18 Dance Tunes from Caslav Region for
Ukulele with low G
10 songs from the years 1899-1920 for
Ukulele with low G
Czech Hymnbook for Ukulele with low G
Boogie woogie patterns for ukulele with
low G
Compositions for ukulele with low G
Second Fingerpicking solo for Ukulele
with low G
Double Stop Gospel for Ukulele
with low G

For Baritone ukulele
Irish tunes for all ukulele
Gospel Baritone Ukulele Solos
Antonin Dvorak: Biblical Songs: for Bari-
tone Ukulele
Gregorian chant for Baritone Ukulele
The Czech Lute for Baritone Ukulele
Romantic Pieces by Frantisek Max Knize
for Baritone Ukulele
Notebook for Anna Magdalena Bach and
Baritone Ukulele
Robert Burns songs for Baritone ukulele
Jewish songs for baritone ukulele
Campanella style songbook for beginner:
Baritone ukulele
Czech Medieval Baritone Ukulele
Christmas Carols for Baritone ukulele
Fingerpicking solo for Baritone ukulele
43 Ghiribizzi by Niccolo Paganini for
Baritone ukulele
Christmas Carols for Crosspicking
Baritone ukulele
Czech Renaissance folk songs for
Baritone ukulele

Gospel Crosspicking Baritone Ukulele
Solos
Josef Pekárek Two Hanakian operas for
Baritone Ukulele
18 Dance Tunes from Caslav Region for
Baritone Ukulele
10 songs from the years 1899-1920 for
Baritone Ukulele
Czech Hymnbook for Baritone Ukulele
Boogie woogie patterns for
Baritone Ukulele
Compositions for Baritone Ukulele
Second Fingerpicking solo for
Baritone Ukulele
Double Stop Gospel for Baritone Ukulele

For Baritone ukulele with high D
Jewish songs for baritone ukulele
with high D
Campanella style songbook for beginner:
Baritone ukulele with high D
Solo and Variations for Baritone ukulele
with high D volume 1., 2., 3.

For 6 sting ukulele (Liliʻu ukulele)
Gospel 6 string Ukulele Solos
Gregorian chant for 6 string Ukulele
Notebook for Anna Magdalena Bach and 6
string Ukulele
Robert Burns songs for 6 string ukulele

For Slide ukulele (lap steel ukulele)
Comprehensive Slide Ukulele: Guidance
for Slide Ukulele Playing
Gospel Slide Ukulele Solos
Irish tunes for slide ukulele
Robert Burns songs for Slide ukulele

For D tuning ukulele
Skola hry na ukulele (G+W s.r.o.)
Irish tunes for all ukulele (CSI)
Jewish songs for D tuning ukulele (CSI)
Campanella style songbook for beginner:
D tuning ukulele (CSI)

Guitalele (Guitarlele)
Fingerpicking Guitalele Solo volume I. -IV.
Gregorian chant for Guitalele
The Czech Lute for Guitalele
Irish tunes for Guitalele
The canons for Guitalele
Gospel Guitalele Solos
Fingerpicking Guitalele Solo volume V. - Classical music
Czech Medieval Guitalele
Czech Renaissance folk songs for Guitalele

Robert Burns songs for Guitalele
18 Dance Tunes from Caslav Region for Guitalele
Czech Hymnbook for Guitalele
18 popular Czech Minuet for Guitalele

For EADA tuning ukulele
EADA ukulele tuning
Gospel EADA Ukulele Solos

Ukulele Duets

Notebook for Anna Magdalena Bach, C tuning ukulele and C tuning ukulele
Notebook for Anna Magdalena Bach, C tuning ukulele and Ukulele with low G
Notebook for Anna Magdalena Bach, C tuning ukulele and Baritone ukulele
Notebook for Anna Magdalena Bach, Ukulele with low G and Ukulele with low G
Notebook for Anna Magdalena Bach, Ukulele with low G and

Baritone ukulele
Notebook for Anna Magdalena Bach, Baritone ukulele and Baritone ukulele
The canons for one or two ukuleles
Mauro Giuliani arranged for Ukulele Duet (MB)
Notebook for Anna Magdalena Bach for Ukulele and EADGBE Guitar
Notebook for Wolfgang for Ukulele and EADGBE Guitar

New Diatonic Accordion (Melodeon) books
For G/C diatonic accordion
Bass songbook for G/C melodeon
Cross row style songbook for beginner G/C diatonic accordion
Gospel G/C diatonic accordion Solos
9 songs from the years 1899-1920 for G/C melodeon
Czech Hymnbook for G/C melodeon
Songbook for G/C diatonic accordion *Volume 1. -2.*
18 popular Czech Minuet for G/C diatonic accordion
Robert Burns songs for G/C diatonic accordion
Jewish songs for G/C diatonic accordion

For C/F diatonic accordion
Cross row style songbook for beginner C/F diatonic accordion
Gospel C/F diatonic accordion Solos
9 songs from the years 1899-1920 for C/F melodeon

For D/G diatonic accordion
Cross row style songbook for beginner

D/G diatonic accordion
Gospel D/G diatonic accordion Solos
9 songs from the years 1899-1920 for D/G melodeon
Robert Burns songs for D/G diatonic accordion

New Anglo Concertina books

For C/G 30-button Wheatstone Lachenal System
Gospel Anglo Concertina Solos
Notebook for Anna Magdalena Bach and Anglo Concertina
Robert Burns songs for Anglo Concertina
The Czech Lute for Anglo Concertina
Gregorian chant for Anglo Concertina
Josef Pekárek *Two Hanakian operas* for Anglo Concertina

For C/G 20-button
Gospel C/G Anglo Concertina Solos
Robert Burns songs for C/G Anglo Concertina
Gregorian chant for Anglo Concertina

Kalimba
Songbook for Kalimba B11 Melody
Second songbook for Kalimba B11 Melody
Songbooks for Kalimba Am+G
Czech Hymnbook for Alto *Hugh Tracey* Kalimba

Robert Burns songs for Alto *Hugh Tracey* Kalimba
Songbooks for Kalimba E116
Songbooks for Alto *Hugh Tracey* Kalimba
Jewish songs for Alto Hugh Tracey Kalimba
Gospel songs for Alto Hugh Tracey Kalimba

New Flute Recorder books
18 Dance Tunes from Caslav Region for Recorder Quartet
Josef Pekárek Two Hanakian operas for Recorder Quartet

Czech Medieval Songs For Two Recorders
Robert Burns songs for Recorder Quartet

Publishing House
CSI = CreateSpace Independent Publishing Platform
MB = Mel Bay Publications
G+W = G+W s.r.o.

Printed in Great Britain
by Amazon

79360987R00025